MW00479867

Geopolitics of Outer Space:
Global Security and Development

A Senior Essay Presented to the Faculty of the
Department of Political Science, Colorado College,
In Partial Fulfillment of the Requirements for the
Degree of Bachelor of Arts, Spring 2018

GEOPOLITICS

OF

OUTER SPACE

GLOBAL SECURITY
AND DEVELOPMENT

ILAYDA AYDIN

Westphalia Press
An Imprint of the Policy Studies Organization
Washington, DC
2019

GEOPOLITICS OF OUTER SPACE:
GLOBAL SECURITY AND DEVELOPMENT

All Rights Reserved © 2019 by Policy Studies Organization

Westphalia Press
An imprint of Policy Studies Organization
1527 New Hampshire Ave., NW
Washington, D.C. 20036
info@ipsonet.org

ISBN-10: 1-63391-827-0
ISBN-13: 978-1-63391-827-6

Cover and interior design by Jeffrey Barnes
jbarnesbook.design

Daniel Gutierrez-Sandoval, Executive Director
PSO and Westphalia Press

Updated material and comments on this edition
can be found at the Westphalia Press website:
www.westphaliapress.org

Many thanks to:

Professor David Hendrickson for his help and support, and to Doctor Hasan Yesiloglu for his contributions.

For my family

CONTENTS:

I. INTRODUCTION:

The past two decades of U.S.–China relations in space point toward heightened competition and hostility. Such behavior consists of increased militarization and antagonism which pose a threat to the security imperatives of all spacefaring bodies. As commercial and military space programs complement each other more and more each day, it is of crucial importance for states to acknowledge and accommodate the environmental and political realities of an increasingly congested and contested environment. Some scholars argue that space would be best utilized as a sanctuary while others argue for its militarization. "Space sanctuary" encompasses *global interactionism and social interactionism*—which mainly grounds in Kantian ideas of universalist thinking. "Space defense," on the other hand, encompasses ideas of *space nationalism and technological determinism*—whose foundations lay in the ideas of Thucydides, Machiavelli and Hobbes. This school of thinking anticipates an inherent state of war, mitigated through *realpolitik.* This essay argues that ideas of "space defense," manifesting as militarization and weaponization of space assets, undermine the developmental and security potential of the domain. The Chinese–American discourse exemplifies the geopolitical informants of space policy while illustrating the classical security dilemma in which existential mantras justify defensive actions. This essay investigates whether space development furthers or undermines global security, in an effort to argue that an obsession with security might pose an ironically existential threat to spacefaring states and the greater humanity in this most fragile yet unforgiving environment. The real challenge for the future is to overcome environmental limitations, and to effectively utilize space by coordinating actors.

II. AN OVERVIEW OF THE AMERICAN AND CHINESE SPACE PROGRAMS:

i. Space Program of the United States of America:

The Department of Defense (DoD) and National Aeronautics and Space Administration (NASA), respectively, conduct the military and civil space programs of the United States. The two institutions cooperatively develop and operate systems for communications satellites, positioning, navigation and timing satellites, early warning, weather, ballistic missile defense-related, launch vehicles, space situational awareness, space control, and operationally responsive space programs. The United States, with its various state departments, commercial partnerships and annual budget, is by far the main space power. In line with the preceding years, its military and intelligence space spending constituted 59% of institutional space spending worldwide in 2008, amounting to more than 66 billion U.S. dollars despite the crippling financial crisis.[1] That number encompassed 17.3 billion U.S. dollars for NASA and an estimated 47.8 billion U.S. dollars for military space programs. In 2016, DoD's budget accounted for 66.7% (or an estimated $22.00 billion) of the global space security expenses and was used by the DoD and its informants: National Reconnaissance Office, National Oceanic and Atmospheric Administration, Department of Energy, Federal Aviation Administration, National Science Foundation, Federal Communications Commission, United States Geological Survey.[2] Although political disputes such as presidential campaigns, congressional hearings etc. had

---

1   Schrogl, K., Blandina, B., Christophe, V., & Wolfgang, R. (Eds.), *Yearbook on Space Policy 2008/2009: Setting New Trends* (Springer-Verlag Wien, 2010), p. 44.

2   Al-Ekabi, C., & Ferretti, S. (Eds.), *Yearbook on Space Policy 2016: Space for Sustainable Development* (Springer International Publishing, 2018), p. 84.

impacts on the nature of projects pursued, the United States has not ceased to account for more than 50% of the worldwide spending on space programs since the Cold War.

ii. Space Policy of the United States:

National Space Policy (NSP), which was issued by President Barack Obama and his administration in 2010, provides guidance to the concerned agencies of the United States on issues pertaining to the economic, strategic, military, civil and developmental aspects of space affairs. It suggests "(i) the enhancement of security, stability, and responsible behavior in space (ii) promotion of the adoption of policies internationally that facilitate full, open, and timely access to government environmental data (iii) promotion of appropriate cost- and risk-sharing among participating nations in international partnerships, and development of transparency and confidence building measures."[3] It acknowledges the need for international cooperation over research and development efforts as well as security concerns such as debris monitoring and awareness, missile warning, and long-term preservation of the space environment for human activity and use. It puts particular stress on reassuring U.S. allies of commitment to collective self-defense as well as the identification of areas of mutual interest and benefit. It outlines a vision of action that is grounded in the interoperability of U.S. commercial space regulations with international regulations. The policy considers the development and use of nuclear power systems where "such systems safely enable or significantly enhance space exploration or operational capabilities,"[4] and authorizes the president and his designee to launch

---

3   The White House, "National Space Policy of the United States of America," June 28, 2010, available at <https://www.nasa.gov/sites/default/files/national_space_policy_6-28-10.pdf>, pp. 11–12.

4   Ibid., p. 8.

these systems. It demands that such a decision be informed by the Secretary of Energy via the Interagency Nuclear Safety Review Panel.

From 2011 to 2018, the NSP informed the National Security Space Strategy (NSSS) which outlined the national strategic approach to the maintenance and enhancement of national security benefits derived from space activities and capabilities. It highlighted the promotion of responsible, peaceful and safe use of space through both national and international organizations in a "congested, contested, and competitive environment."[5] The strategy gave a broad framework on how to prevent, deter, and defeat aggression through a multilayered approach that unfolds as:

> support diplomatic efforts to promote norms of responsible behavior in space; pursue international partnerships that encourage potential adversary restraint; improve our ability to attribute attacks; strengthen the resilience of our architectures to deny the benefits of an attack; and retain the right to respond, should deterrence fail.[6]

As the first step of deterrence, the NSSS pursued "the denial of meaningful benefits of an attack to adversaries who seek counterspace actions for military advantage."[7] While renouncing the belief that avoiding hostilities in space is in the interest of all space-faring nations, it retained the right and capabilities to respond in self-defense to fight through a degraded environment.

---

5   Department of Defense, "National Security Space Strategy Unclassified Summary," January 2011, available at <https://www.dni.gov/files/documents/Newsroom/Reports%2and%20Pubs/2011_nationalsecurity spacestrategy.pdf>, p. 1.

6   Ibid., p. 10.

7   Ibid.

In March 2018, President Trump issued an "America First National Space Strategy" statement that replaced the Obama-era NSSS.[8] The updated strategy corresponds to the thematic transformation under the Trump administration, and "prioritizes American interests first and foremost, ensuring a strategy that will make America strong, competitive, and great." [9] It ensures that "international agreements put the interests of American people, workers, and businesses first" and "prioritizes regulatory reforms that will unshackle American industry and ensure [that Americans] remain the leading global provider of space services and technology." In essence, the paper doesn't differ from the 2011 NSSS in its methods for development, cooperation, defense or deterrence in space. It prioritizes securing the scientific, commercial, and national security benefits of space while promising to continue to lead in the creation and maintenance of space systems that are essential to American prosperity, security, and way of life.[10] However, it highlights one very distinct characteristic of the Trump administration and the contemporary American political discourse: nationalism. With consideration of the economic and technological advantages to the state, the Trump administration prioritizes the development of American commercial industry to increase market share and intellectual property rights. The administration has already endorsed commercialization recommendations such as licensing to enhance the role of the Office of Space Commerce within the

8   Space Policy Online, "Military/National Security Space Activities," March 2018, available at <https://spacepolicyonline.com/topics/militarynational-security-space-activities/#policy1>

9   The White House, "President Donald J. Trump Is Unveiling an America First National Space Strategy," March 23, 2018, available at <http://www.whitehouse.gov/briefings-statements/president-donald-j-trump-unveiling-america-first-national-space-strategy/>

10 Ibid.

Department of Commerce.[11] $150 million of the 2019 budget is allocated to encourage private development of low-Earth orbit missions with SpaceX, Orbital ATK, Sierra Nevada, Boeing and Axiom Space. Simultaneously, to fund new initiatives, NASA will end its $1.5 billion support of the International Space Station by 2025.[12] Such development does not suggest drastic changes in security interests per se, but does highlight priorities in both domestic and foreign policy. The new strategy factsheet recognizes space as a "warfighting domain" and "affirms that any harmful interference with or attack upon critical components of [American] space architecture that directly affects [any] vital interest will be met with a deliberate response at a time, place, manner, and domain of [American] choosing." The tone and attitude of the new strategy is strikingly aggressive when compared with the 2011 NSSS. While having similar security concerns with the old policy, the drastic changes in the outlook of space conduct under the Trump administration flags U.S. international engagement with a red flag for caution. Moreover, it prompts foreign nations to develop counter-strategic doctrines, methods and measures.

On June 30, 2017, the President revived the National Space Council for the first time in 24 years to hint at a further revision of space policy. In March 2018, Trump introduced the possibility of creating a Space Force, which would operate separately from the Air Force to address the needs of this "war-fighting domain" that is increasingly more vulnerable to

---

11 Foust, Jeff. "New National Space Strategy Emphasizes 'America First' Policies," *Space News*, March 24, 2018, available at <https://spacenews.com/new-national-space-strategy-emphasizes-america-first-policies/>

12 Amadeo, Kimberly. "NASA Budget, Current Funding, and History," *The Balance*, March 24, 2018, available at <https://www.thebalance.com/nasa-budget-current-funding-and-history-3306321>

attacks. Currently, the U.S. government is working to make significant improvements in joint interoperability and lethality capabilities for its attack reconnaissance aircrafts, in airborne weapons systems and missiles, in the radiation belt specification of space vehicles, and in incorporating new software and hardware to better acquire littoral and unmanned aircraft system (UAS) targets for proximity fuse and fragmentation capability.[13] Since late 2017, the Space Warfighting Construct is working to combine transformational and warfighting-focused command initiatives,[14] to transform space into "a more robust and resilient architecture to maintain space superiority in the 21st century."[15] Moreover, the National Defense Authorization Act (NDAA) for Fiscal Year 2018 is laying the foundation of reorganized and consolidated space capabilities to deliver "persistent [and] critical warfighting capabilities."[16] American attention to and awareness of the military strategic, economic and political benefits of space development is conspicuously leading to a militarized space with antagonistic national programs.

iii. Space Program of the People's Republic of China:

The Chinese National Space Administration (CNSA) is the second biggest national space program after the United States',

---

13 National Aeronautics and Space Administration (NASA), "Aeronautics and Space Report of the President, Fiscal Year 2016 Activities," June 12, 2017, available at <https://history.nasa.gov/presrep2016.pdf>

14 Merian, 1st Lt. Christopher. "AFSPC commander unveils three major space initiatives at 33rd Space Symposium," *Headquarters Air Force Space Command Public Affairs*, April 7, 2017, available at <http://www.afspc.af.mil/News/Article-Display/Article/1145448/afspc-commander-unveils-three-major-space-initiatives-at-33rd-space-symposium/>

15 Cowen-Hirsh, Rebecca. "Leadership and Industry Development Pave a New Path for Unified SATCOM," *Milsat Magazine* (April 2018): p. 26.

16 Ibid.

and is likely larger than the modest estimate of $4.22 billion.[17,18] CNSA successfully conducted manned space launches, a landing on the moon, and manned dockings in space. It also successfully completed an anti-satellite test in 2007.[19] In 2016, it launched 22 vehicles—same amount as the United States, and is continuing to ramp up its space plans, including a Mars rover mission set to launch in 2020.[20] As part of the 13th five-year plan, CNSA's Mars Exploration Project is officially approved, the National Civil Space Infrastructure Construction is established, the moon-bound Chang'e-4 mission is initiated, the Chang'e-5 lunar project entered a key stage, and the Beidou Navigation System accelerated integration with global networking.[21] Along with the "non-poisonous and pollution-free" Long March 5 and 7 boosters' maiden flights, CNSA is planning many major events in 2018.[22] CNSA is not affiliated with the International Space Station, and uses its own small station in orbit to facilitate its space activity. This fell on April 1, 2018.

---

17 Al-Ekabi, *Yearbook on Space Policy 2016: Space for Sustainable Development*, p. 48.

18 That is around 14% of NASA's budget for the 2018 fiscal year. The CNSA is aiming to triple that number to an approximate of $12.6 billion USD by 2026. For more, see Echo Huang, "China's Fallen Space Lab Was a Prism for Its Space Ambitions," *Quartz*, March 26, 2018, available at <https://qz.com/1232198/tiangong-1-chinas-falling-space-lab-is-a-prism-for-its-space-ambitions/?utm_source=atlfb>

19 Howell, Elizabeth. "China National Space Administration: Facts & Information," *Space.com*, May 25, 2016, available at <https://www.space.com/22743-china-national-space-administration.html>

20 Huang, Echo. "China's Fallen Space Lab Was a Prism for Its Space Ambitions," *Quartz*, March 26, 2018, available at <https://qz.com/1232198/tiangong-1-chinas-falling-space-lab-is-a-prism-for-its-space-ambitions/?utm_source=atlfb>

21 Central Committee of the Communist Party of China, "The 13th Five-Year Plan for Economic and Social Development of the People's Republic of China (2016–2020)," March 2016, available at <http://en.ndrc.gov.cn/newsrelease/201612/P020161207645765233498.pdf>

22 David, Leonard. "China to Launch Mars Rover in 2020," *Space.com*, April

China abides by the United Nations (UN) Committee on the Peaceful Uses of Outer Space and all UN treaties and conventions on space, besides the 1979 Moon Treaty.[23] It has in place more than 100 cooperation agreements signed with 30 state-level space institutions and international organizations.[24]

iv. Space Policy of the People's Republic of China:

The 2015 Middle and Long Term Development Plan for State Civil Space Infrastructure (2015–2025) of China announces the objectives of improving space infrastructure and competitiveness as to enhance state capability for domestic purposes.[25] China's Space Activities in 2016 further outlines the purposes of space development as:

> to explore outer space and enhance understanding of the earth and the cosmos; to utilize outer space for peaceful purposes, promote human civilization and social progress, and benefit the whole of mankind; to meet the demands of economic, scientific and technological development, national security and social progress; and to improve the scientific and cultural levels of the Chinese people, protect China's national rights and interests, and build up its overall strength.[26]

27, 2016, available at <https://www.space.com/32715-china-mars-moon-exploration-plans.html>

23 United Nations Committee on the Peaceful Uses of Outer Space, "Status of International Agreements relating to activities in outer space as at January 1, 2014," March 20, 2014, available at <http://www.unoosa.org/pdf/limited/c2/AC105_C2_2014_CRP07E.pdf>

24 David, "China to Launch Mars Rover in 2020."

25 The State Council Information Office of the People's Republic of China, "China's Space Activities in 2016," December 27, 2017, available at <http://english.scio.gov.cn/2017-01/10/content_40535777.htm>

26 The State Council of the People's Republic of China, "White Paper on China's

While highlighting domestic development and publicly oppos-
ing the militarization of space, the 2015 white paper on China's
Military Strategy adds a military layer to the Chinese space en-
deavor. It establishes a guideline of *active defense* with stronger
capabilities for strategic deterrence, nuclear counterattack, and
medium- and long-range precision strikes.[27] The document defines active defense as striking a balance between rights protection and stability maintenance, making serious preparations to
cope with the most complex and difficult scenarios, bringing
into full play the unique political advantages of the people's
armed forces, giving full play to the overall power of the concept of people's war.[28] It also announces the optimization of
nuclear force structure for the improvement of strategic early
warning, command and control, missile penetration, rapid reaction, survivability and protection, and deterrence systems.
Importantly, the strategy envisions to realize "the Chinese
Dream of the renewal of the Chinese nation."[29] Such a "dream"
pertains to economic and social construction, and firm maintenance of social stability "so as to remain a staunch force
for upholding the CPC's ruling position and a reliable force
for developing socialism with Chinese characteristics."[30] The
white paper attributes the realization to strategic deployment
and military disposition "to maintain the common security of

Space Activities in 2016," December 28, 2016, available at <http://english.
gov.cn/archive/white_paper/2016/12/28/content_281475527159496.
htm>, p. 1

27 Al-Ekabi, *Yearbook on Space Policy 2016*, p. 88.

28 Ministry of National Defense of the People's Republic of China, "China's
Military Strategy," May 26, 2015, available at <http://eng.mod.gov.cn/
Press/2015-05/26/content_4586805_6.htm>, p. 3.

29 Ibid., p. 2.

30 People's Liberation Army, "China's Military Strategy," *China Military Online*, May 26, 2015, available at <http://english.chinamil.com.cn/news-
channels/2015-05/26/content_6507716_2.htm>, p. 2.

the world community" before threats from traditional and new security domains such as outer space and cyber space.[31] Over all, the white paper provides a military dimension to Chinese security strategy and in doing so avoids offensive alternatives. In fact, it stresses that "China always adheres to the principle of the use of outer space for peaceful purposes, and opposes the weaponization of or an arms race in outer space."[32] It lists the improvement of bilateral cooperation with Russia, the ESA, Brazil, United States, and multilateral cooperation through the UN, APSCO, BRICS, IADC, and ICG as its major successes.

---

31 Ibid., p. 3.

32 "White Paper on China's Space Activities in 2016," p. 1.

III. THE U.S.–CHINA INTERPLAY:

The U.S. government responded to the 9/11 attacks with hyper securitizing its strategic frontier. As the event confronted the nation with its international dependency and vulnerability, policy-makers assumed a self-mandate for dramatic change in foreign policy.[1] Concluding that "nuclear deterrence wasn't a guarantee of strategic invulnerability," the military–industrial complex turned to realism for their policy on space development.[2] The government identified security threats beyond the protection of the 1972 Anti-Ballistic Missile Treaty (ABM), and isolated its security concerns from those of other states'.[3] The United States withdrew from the ABM treaty on December 13, 2001,[4] announcing that the treaty "hinders [the American government's] ability to develop ways to protect [American] people from future terrorist or rogue-state missile attacks."[5] This development created a wave of anxiety in the international arena. It also reminded that all nations are free, to the degree of their security capacity, to act unilaterally. Russian President Putin immediately responded to the withdrawal as "a mistake."[6] Soon after that, Russia announced that it would not abide by

---

1   Moltz, J.C. *The Politics of Space Security: Strategic Restraint and the Pursuit of National Interests* (Stanford, CA: Stanford University Press, 2011), p. 259.

2   Grondin, David. *Securing Outer Space*. Ed. Natalie Bormann (London: Routledge, 2009), p. 109.

3   Moltz, *The Politics of Space Security*, p. 259.

4   "The Outer Space Treaty outlined four basic concepts: the parties agreed to keep space open for exploration and use by all states, take responsibility for all activities conducted from within their borders (whether carried out by governmental or nongovernmental entities), assume liability for damage caused by their space objects, and cooperate with one another and provide mutual assistance." Baiocchi, D., & Welser, W., IV. (2015). The Democratization of Space: New Actors Need New Rules. *Foreign Affairs, 94*(3), 98–104.

5   Moltz, *The Politics of Space Security*, p. 269.

6   Ibid.

the START II agreement, which would require the dismantling of all land-based, multiple-warhead missiles. The country also raised barriers on the Joint Data Exchange Center (JDEC) and the Russian American Satellite (RAMOS) project.[7] The Bush administration announced that such a reaction was expected and that the United States will continue developing its defensive capacity. The following years were marked by intensive development of Space-Based Infrared Systems, High and Low early warning systems, Theater High Altitude Area Defense systems, Space-Based Laser systems, space-based kinetic-kill interceptors for long-range missiles, and several more.[8]

In April 2001, a Chinese jet fighter and a U.S. Navy spy plane crashed about 50 miles southeast of China's Hainan island—which is considered to be "international waters" by U.S. officials.[9] The crash was followed by the American plane's landing on the island and the Chinese jet's crashing into the waters. An expert on the Chinese military at George Washington University, David Shambaugh explained that the plane was "a sophisticated surveillance aircraft ... that is loaded with electronic surveillance gear that can hear and see into the mainland."[10] It was unclear whether there was any intelligence collected during the flight, but it spoke to the fears of the Chinese government. Moreover, the timing was uncanny, as President Bush was to decide on a big arms deal with Taiwan in a few weeks. The Chinese government demanded the United States to take full responsibility of the event and the damages associ-

---

7   Moltz, *The Politics of Space Security,* p. 272.

8   Ibid.

9   Rosenthal, E., & Sanger D.E., "U.S. Plane in China After It Collides with Chinese Jet," *The New York Times,* April 2, 2001, available at <https://www.nytimes.com/2001/04/02/world/us-plane-in-china-after-it-collides-with-chinese-jet.html>

10 Ibid.

ated. Many scholars alluded to the accidental bombing of the Chinese Embassy in Belgrade by NATO forces in 1999, where the line between accident and agenda was blurred, while agitation was certain. Assuredly, neither the death of a Chinese pilot nor the detention of American staff were perceived well by their respective governments. If anything, the accident fueled ongoing distrust in intentions. China's Ambassador to the UN Hu Xiaodi, in October 2001, warned that, "[U.S. space policy] is rather the attempt toward the domination of outer space, which is expected to serve in turn the absolute security and perpetual superiority (many people call this hegemony) of one country on earth. The unilateralism and exceptionalism that are on the rise in recent months also mutually reinforce this."[11] A year after, in December 2002, the United States deployed a ballistic missile defense system to create an *active defense* measure that allows for protection and pre-emptive attacks.[12] It was followed by a doubling of missile defense spending, and the enunciation of broad plans for space weapons for both defensive and offensive capabilities. Despite the budgetary deficit due to ongoing wars and increasing military competition, the administration refused to impose financial restrictions, and only implemented voluntary guidelines on the development of military capacity—in effect, encouraging further militarization.[13] Meanwhile, the Commission to Assess United States National Security Space Management and Organization pointed to the absence of a prohibitive international law on placing weapons in space, and called for the development of effective systems to avoid a "Space Pearl

---

11 Podvig, Pavel, & Hui, Zhang. "Russian and Chinese Responses to U.S. Military Plans in Space, Chapter 2," *American Academy of Arts & Sciences*, March 2008, available at <https://www.amacad.org/content/publications/pubContent.aspx?d=1201>

12 Grondin, *Securing Outer Space*, p. 200.

13 Moltz, *The Politics of Space Security*, p. 260.

Harbor."[14] As distrust and discord continued to grow among states, the Airforce Vision of 2020 was announced to be the construction of "a seamless web of land-based, sea-based, air-based, and space-based systems that would allow the United States to achieve 'full spectrum' of dominance."[15,16] Simultaneously, the possibility of China's asymmetric use of nuclear weapons in space began echoing in the military-intelligence chambers of the United States.[17] In 2002, Representative Shaffer charged China with having a "strategic alliance with Saddam Hussein" while offering no evidence.[18] The same year, in March, the Pentagon successfully tested another ground-based interceptor.[19] A month later, Chinese Vice Foreign Minister Qiao Zonghuai commented that,

> It will not take long before drawings of space weapons and weapon systems [are] turned into lethal combat instruments in outer space. Meanwhile, military doctrines and [concepts] such as "control of space" and "ensuring space superiority" have been unveiled successively, and space operation [command] headquarters and combatant troops are in the making. If we should remain indifferent to the above-mentioned developments, an arms race would very likely emerge in outer space in the foreseeable future. Outer space would eventually become the fourth battlefield besides land, sea and air. If such a scenario should

---

14 Moltz, *The Politics of Space Security*, p. 262.

15 Ibid.

16 United States Department of Air Force, "America's Air Force Vision 2020," 2000, available at <http://webapp1.dlib.indiana.edu/virtual_disk_library/index.cgi/4240529/FID3869/pdfdocs/2020/afvision.pdf>, p. 2.

17 Moltz, *The Politics of Space Security*, p. 163.

18 Moltz, *The Politics of Space Security*, p. 270.

19 Ibid.

become reality it would be virtually impossible for mankind to continue their anticipated exploration, development and utilization of outer space, and all economic, cultural and social activities in connection with the utilization of outer space would be severely interrupted.[20]

In December, the updated U.S. Nuclear Posture Review stated that "missile defense is most effective if it is layered; that is, able to intercept ballistic missiles of any range in all phases of their flight."[21] This statement effectively announced the inclusion of space-based sensors, early-warning satellites, space tracking, and surveillance systems to the U.S. missions.[22] 2002 and 2003 witnessed increasing budgets and massive congressional debates on the defense and foreign policy. In 2003, China successfully launched its first taikonaut Yang Liwei—a few months after the failure of the U.S. space shuttle Columbia that killed seven astronauts and the first Israeli in space.[23] China also received significant developmental support from Russia, and demonstrated early stages of cooperation in space—which only contributed to anxieties within the United States. Yet, the Bush administration zealously declined any opportunity for the two countries to cooperate. The same year, the U.S. Air Force's Transformation Flight Plan listed a number of space weapon systems desirable in the event of a

20 Zonghuai, Qiao. "An Effective Way to Prevent an Arms Race in Outer Space the Early Negotiation and Conclusion of an International Legal Instrument," speech presented at the China/UN Disarmament Conference, April 3, 2002, available at <http://www3.fmprc.gov.cn/eng/29794.html>

21 The United States Department of Defense, "Excerpts of Classified Nuclear Posture Review," *Nuclear Posture Review Report*, December 31, 2001, available at <https://fas.org/wp-content/uloads/media/Excerpts-of-Classified-Nuclear-Posture-Review.pdf>.

22 Podvig, "Russian and Chinese Responses to U.S. Military Plans in Space."

23 Moltz, *The Politics of Space Security*, p. 275.

space war.[24] In 2004, Bush made a call for U.S. space programs to catch up with other nations', and accelerate the Moon and Mars projects.[25] Soon after, China announced that it is ready to recalibrate its stance at a time where "Washington's position diverged so far from international opinion that these compromises failed" to make sense.[26] China and Russia turned to develop their space technologies while pushing for international consensus on space conduct, including a ban on the weaponization of space. In 2006, the governments of China and Russia introduced the draft text of an international treaty to the Conference of Disarmament (CD) which didn't receive a positive response from the United States.[27] Russian Ambassador to the CD called the ambitions to achieve domination in space "illusory" and threatening to all states' security.

The following years, George W. Bush's second term, were marked by drastic changes in the Chinese space policy. From 2007 onwards, Chinese efforts for international cooperation and a treaty to ban space weapons was coupled with strong efforts to improve weapons technology. The double-edged character of the new Chinese policy, preparing for conflict both in the diplomatic and military realms, began hinting at the state's perception of inevitable conflict. In 2007, six years after the American withdrawal from the ABM treaty, China tested an anti-satellite (ASAT) weapon on one of its own satellites. The test was controversial in two ways: it was conducted just a few days after a significant U.S.–Taiwan arms deal, and it vi-

---

24 Podvig, "Russian and Chinese Responses to U.S. Military Plans in Space."

25 National Aeronautics and Space Administration (NASA), "President Bush Delivers Remarks on U.S. Space Policy," January 14, 2004, available at <https://www.nasa.gov/pdf/54868main_bush_trans.pdf>

26 Moltz, *The Politics of Space Security*, p. 281.

27 United Nations Office for Disarmament Affairs (UNODA), "Outer Space," available at <https://www.un.org/disarmament/topics/outerspace/>

olated the norm of no-destructive ASAT testing for the first time since the American test in 1985.[28] The U.S perceived it as a direct threat since the destroyed satellite was orbiting at the same altitude with many U.S. spy satellites.[29] Increasing defensive measures did not only confront the possibility of similar testing efforts worldwide, but also highlighted shared security threats in space such as increasing space debris. As mirror-imaging in international affairs uncannily resembled the faulty notions of stability and assured deterrence of the Cold War era, space warfare became a growing international fear. As much as Chinese technology was outstandingly simpler than that of *Soyuz* '67, back in 2007,[30] a growing number of Chinese publications began to indicate that China might proceed with the principle that its sovereign territorial airspace extends through outer space (Stone, 2016). In fact, China began to effectively use the holes in international legislature with the claim that "territorial claims to outer space are not inconsistent with international law because there is no legally accepted definition of 'outer space' that defines the demarcation point at which territorial airspace ends and outer space begins."[31] The documentation by Pentagon of a growing investment pattern in satellite communications, satellite navigation, intelligence surveillance and reconnaissance (ISR) furthered U.S. security concerns.[32]

---

28 Kakaes, K. "Weapons in Space," *CQ Global Researcher*, Issue 5, August 16, 2011, available at <http://library.cqpress.com/cqresearcher/document.php?id=cqrglobal2011081600>

29 Oh, Paul. "Assessing Chinese Intentions for the Military Use of the Space Domain," *Joint Forces Quarterly*, Issue 64, 1st Quarter, January 2012, <http://www.dtic.mil/dtic/tr/fulltext/u2/a575520.pdf>, p. 95.

30 Ibid., p. 96.

31 Stone, C. "The Implications of Chinese Strategic Culture and Counter-Intervention upon Department of Defense Space Deterrence Operations," *Comparative Strategy*, December 7, 2016, <https://doi.org/10.1080/01495933.2016.1240964>, p. 336.

32 Moltz, *The Politics of Space Security*, p.

After the ASAT test, "space leaders within DoD immediately called out for new systems with the capabilities commanders need to protect the nation's critical space inventory."[33] American military strategists saw the ASAT test as a "critical element of a robust space deterrent that can further protect China's nuclear and conventional deterrents against emerging threats like US ballistic missile defense programs."[34] The same strategists also drew three guiding assumptions from the Chinese test:

(i) *China's stated commitment to a negotiated space treaty is unreliable.*

(ii) *China appreciates the strategic deterrent value of antisatellite weapons*

(iii) *China aspires for greater relevance within the international space community.*[35]

In October 2008, Russia and China jointly proposed a treaty to ban weapons in space. While seeming to advocate for an updated legal instrument that could address emerging challenges, the Russian–Chinese draft was found inadequate by the U.S. delegation as it was "not possible" to define what a space-based weapon is.[36] "Proposed arms control agreements or restrictions must not impair the rights of the US to conduct research, development, testing and operation or other activities in space for US national interests," declared the White House spokes-

---

33 Mastalir, Anthony J. *The US Response to China's ASAT Test: An International Security Space Alliance for the Future* (Air University Press, 2009), available at <www.jstor.org/stable/resrep13986>, p. 2.

34 Ibid., p. 4.

35 Ibid., p. 6.

36 United Nations General Assembly, "Preventing Outer Space Arms Race Would Avert Grave Danger; Possible New Verifiable Bilateral Multilateral Agreements Needed, Says Draft Text in First Committee," October 20, 2008, available at <https://www.un.org/press/en/2008/gadis3371.doc.htm>

woman Dana Perino.[37] In 2008, the United States conducted an operation similar to the 2007 Chinese test, on an American military reconnaissance satellite—USA 193. The satellite had been successfully positioned in the orbit, but control of it had been lost. Although the risk of it falling or causing any damage was identified "extremely low,"[38] President Bush decided that the hydrazine fuel it carried posed too great a threat to human life, and tasked United States Strategic Command to destroy the satellite.[39] In 2010, China conducted a successful land-based missile test involving a new exo-atmospheric kinetic kill vehicle. The test "had a nuanced message" coinciding with the American arms sales to Taiwan and the third year of the ASAT test.[40] It demonstrated "capabilities that match or exceed those of every country in the region besides Russia."[41] The same year, in 2010, the U.S. registered space activity under homeland security in the NSP.[42] China and Russia proposed a revised version of the 2008 treaty to the U.N. in 2014. The U.S. Ambassador Robert Wood found it "fundamentally flawed" like the previous version, and asserted that "we have not yet seen any legally-binding proposals that meet [our] criteria."[43]

---

37 "Russia Proposes Space Weapons Ban," *Al-Jazeera*, February 12, 2008, available at <https://www.aljazeera.com/news/europe/2008/02/2008525132324551376.html>

38 "Decaying Spy Satellite USA 193," *Heavens Above*, available at <http://www.heavens-above.com/usa193.aspx>

39 Blount, P.J., & Gabrynowicz, J.I. (Eds.) "USA-193: Selected Documents," *Serial Topics in Aerospace Law Series 1* (2008), available at <http://www.spacelaw.olemiss.edu/resources/pdfs/usa193-selected-documents.pdf>, p. 63.

40 Oh, Paul. "Assessing Chinese Intentions for the Military Use of the Space Domain," p. 95.

41 Ibid., p. 96.

42 Bowen, B.E. "Cascading Crises: Orbital Debris and the Widening of Space Security." *Astropolitics* 12/1 (March 2014), available at <https://www.tandfonline.com/doi/full/10.1080/14777622.2014.890489>, p. 47.

43 Foust, Jeff. "U.S. Dismisses Space Weapons Treaty Proposal as 'Funda-

The Chinese–American relationship went through considerable changes during the two terms of President Barack Obama—starting with increased bureaucratic exchanges. NASA Administrator Bolden's visit to China led to "a frank discussion of the merits of bilateral cooperation in space."[44] Although Bolden made sure to communicate that the two countries did not need each other for operational purposes, he reported that "the Chinese are eager to cooperate with other spacefaring nations" and the two countries might get somewhere.[45] The visit proved to be a great means to build trust and show willingness to cooperate. Despite democratic barriers in Washington,[46] the administration continued to show its eagerness to improve relations. In 2010, Obama released the NSSS that outlined the U.S. vision for "a secure space environment in which responsible nations have access to space and the benefits of space operations without need to exercise their inherent right of self-defense."[47] 2011 hosted high-level meetings between the DoD and PLA. No immediate results emerged, but a movement of international cooperation was catalyzed. Currently, China and the United States engage in frequent bilateral meetings. In October 2015, the Subgroup on Aviation Augmentations and Applications hosted Chinese and American officials in Washington, DC, to discuss the Chi-

mentally Flawed'," *Space News*, September 11, 2014, available at <http://spacenews.com/41842us-dismisses-space-weapons-treaty-proposal-as-fundamentally-flawed/>

44 Svitak, Amy. "Bolden Details Trip to China During Marshall Visit," *Space News*, November 19, 2010, available at <http://spacenews.com/bolden-details-trip-china-during-marshall-visit/>

45 Ibid.

46 A Republican House of Representative and a nearly Republican Senate that cut NASA's budget, thus disallowed cooperation with China (Moltz, *The Politics of Space Security*, pp. 321–322).

47 The White House, "National Space Policy of the United States of America," p. 4.

nese Satellite Based Augmentation System (SBAS) and other aviation-related topics. In May 2016, a similar bilateral meeting took place on the margins of the China Satellite Navigation Conference in Changsha. In September 2016, the Subgroup on Compatibility and Interoperability brought together Chinese and American officials on the margins of the U.S. Institute of Navigation's GNSS+ 2016 Conference. In June 2016, the Department of State facilitated an Expert Workshop on Satellite Collision Avoidance and Orbital Debris Mitigation with China as a follow up to the first U.S.–China Civil Space Dialogue held in September 2015 in Beijing. Topics of discussion included further collaboration related to space debris and the long-term sustainability of outer space activities, as well as an exchange of views on coordination and communication related to satellite collision avoidance." Obama era policies directed the Chinese–American interplay to a much different and much more hopeful direction than that of the conflict-ridden years following 9/11. However, full cooperation in space remained a work in progress, as the political trust, technical prerequisites, and organizational collaboration for such a transformation of space security does not exist yet.[48]

Since 2007, China has not publicly acknowledged any antisatellite programs—yet, conducted a similar test in 2016. Russia denied a "new Cold War" but announced the development of various advanced missile systems that are responsive to the U.S. withdrawal from the ABM treaty.[49,50] The U.S. responded

---

48 Moltz, *The Politics of Space Security*, p. 323.

49 "Exclusive: Putin blames U.S. for arms race, denies 'new Cold War'," *NBC News*, March 1, 2018, available at <https://www.nbcnews.com/nightly-news/video/exclusive-putin-denies-cold-war-1174558275948>

50 President of Russia, "Presidential Address to the Federal Assembly," March 1, 2018, available at <http://en.kremlin.ru/events/president/news/56957>

as, "Russia has been developing destabilizing weapons systems for over a decade, in direct violation of its treaty obligations."[51] Meanwhile, the Trump administration drastically increased the space budget and ramped up "collaboration between the military and intelligence community on space modernization and strategies to deter and compete against growing space powers like Russia and China."[52] Upon the launch of the SpaceX Falcon Heavy in February, Air Force chief of staff Gen. David Goldfein reported, "It is not a question of if, but when airmen will be fighting in space."[53] Partnership with SpaceX provided the military with economically viable options to construct and operate a new class of vehicles that enable reach anywhere in the world in under an hour.[54] With this new technology, military spaceplanes can now "be launched [by SpaceX] on demand, be fully reusable, turn around in hours and routinely fly to space or overfly any location on Earth."[55] Simultaneously "expandable launch vehicles, reusable systems and next generation spaceplanes—with global reach hypersonic speed, and relative invulnerability"—are being developed for the military by SpaceX, Blue Origin, Boeing and many other companies.[56] Air Force Gen. Hyten and commander of STRATCOM— whose responsibilities include strategic deterrence, nuclear operations, space operations, joint electromagnetic spectrum

---

51 Hodge, N., Starr, B., Chance, M., & Burrows, Emma. "Putin Claims New 'Invincible' Missile Can Pierce US Defenses," *CNN*, March 1, 2018, available at <https://edition.cnn.com/2018/03/01/europe/putin-russia-missile-intl/>

52 Erwin, Sandra. "Military Leaders: National Security Space Shown the Love," April 17, 2018, available at <http://spacenews.com/military-leaders-national-security-space-shown-the-love/>

53 Sponable, Jess. "A Boost for Military Spaceplanes," *Aerospace America* 56/4 (April 2018): p. 32.

54 Ibid., p. 31.

55 Ibid.

56 Ibid., p. 33.

operations, global strike missile defense analysis/targeting and cyberspace operations—testified in March 2018 that "the forces under [his] control are fully ready to deter adversaries and respond decisively, should deterrence fail."[57] Reassuringly, "we are making bold shifts towards war fighting and space superiority," said Air Force Gen. John "Jay" Raymond, commander of Air Force Space Command on April 2018, at the 34th Space Symposium.[58] The White House announced preparations for proposal that plans to "end direct US financial support for the International Space Station in 2025, after which NASA would rely on commercial partners for its low Earth orbit research and technology demonstration requirements."[59] "The administration already requested $12.5 billion in fiscal year 2019 for unclassified national security space—more than $1 billion than it had asked for in 2018. Tens of billions more are in classified budgets."[60] While ramping U.S. military capacity and priming the American innovation scene, it is unclear whether Trump's increasingly isolationist policies will offer United States the security guarantee it seeks.

57 Broadway, Chuck. "STRATCOM Commander Offers Testimony—U.S. Armed Forces Ready to Deter Adversaries," *Milsat Magazine* (April 2018): p. 10.

58 Erwin, "Military Leaders: National Security Space Shown the Love."

59 "Trump Budget Cuts U.S. Cash for International Space Station," *BBC*, February 12, 2018, available at <http://www.bbc.com/news/world-us-canada-43038329>

60 Ibid.

IV. CONTEXT:

i. Space Environment and Geography:

Historically, states join costly technological races depending on prospective gains on security, real or perceived. They use every scintilla of scientific expertise available to them as they seek out the next technology that will change the character of war, and apply full force of government to ensure such scientific efforts aren't available to potential adversaries.[1] Today, space capacity doesn't only enable global telecommunications, geographic extension of services, managing of human resources, navigation, observation and remote sensing, but offers a game-changing strategic advantage to capable actors, and does so exclusively to the fast and the furious. Such strategic advantage would maximize the offensive state's achievements while minimizing the utilization of geographic resources and advantages by its defensive counterpart.[2] However, it depends on the successful utilization of the physical properties and the geographic peculiarities of the space environment.

The first 150–800 km above the surface of the Earth are especially useful for Earth reconnaissance (military observation to include photographic, imaging, and radar satellites as well as resource management satellites) and manned flight missions. These orbits also permit the use of cheaper, less-sophisticated rockets. From 800 km to 35,000 km (circular or low eccentricity orbits) are typically used for linked satellite networks of telecommunications and navigation.[3] From 35,000 km to 700,000 km are ideal for global communications and weather

---

1   Dolman, Everett Carl. *Can Science End War?* (Malden, MA: Polity Press, 2016), p. 6.

2   Dolman, Everett Carl. *Astropolitik: Classical Geopolitics in the Space Age* (Portland, OR: Frank Cass Publishers, 2002), p. 13.

3   Ibid., p. 65.

satellites, as the satellites orbit the earth only once a day and the combined coverage of three satellites provide stable and continuous access.[4] The specific functions of different orbital spaces hold crucial importance for civil, governmental, and military purposes.

As a physical rule, higher altitudes in space are more stable, and orbiting bodies appear to travel slower relative to the bodies they orbit in lower altitudes. This, however, doesn't necessarily mean that higher orbits are more desirable. While higher orbits are advantageous for broader field views, lower orbits provide close-up and detailed views of the Earth and help the maintenance of concentrated low-diffusion communications links. Circular or constant altitude orbits are the most suitable for continuous missions (such as the International Space Station's researches), and eccentric orbits are better for missions that require conduct at critical points in the orbit.[5] Although space can be crossed in any direction, gravity wells and the astronomical costs of fuel transportation to orbits suggest that the future holds heavy traffic around specific orbits and transit routes to reduce costs and increase security.[6] Moreover, the physical forces that cause satellites to gradually change their paths (a.k.a "slip") require additional energy to keep them in their designed orbit.[7] In retrospect, stable orbits are perhaps the most preferable orbits for operational trajectories. The geostationary orbit is a critical operational domain, as the only orbit with a fixed-point capacity.[8] There are five points in the geostationary orbit where the combined gravitational forces of two large bodies, such as Earth and the sun or Earth and the

---

4 Ibid., p. 66.

5 Ibid., pp. 61–64.

6 Ibid., p. 39. 35,000 – 700,000 = Global Comm. + Weather

7 Ibid.

8 Ibid., p. 55. 800, – 35,000 = Communication

150 – 800 km = Recon

moon, create a point of equilibrium where a spacecraft may be "parked" to make observations.[9] These points are called the Lagrange/Lagrarian or liberation points (L). "L-4 and L-5 are located on the same orbital path as the moon and are effectively permanent orbits as the gravitational pulls of the Earth and moon cancel out each other. These two points are ideal for the construction of large-scale orbital infrastructures such as space stations. For their proximity to the earth, they also are perfect points for colonization."[10] "Another such point of stable gravitational equilibrium, L-1, sits a million miles from the Earth and is always situated between the Earth and the sun, making it the preferred location for hypothetical infrastructures to regulate the amount of solar radiation falling on the Earth."[11] In fact, in 2006, NASA placed a satellite at L1, which provided scientists not only with scenic views, but also with metrics on climate such as cloud height, ultraviolet reflectivity, and ozone and aerosol levels. [12]

Outer space, with its many planets, moons, and asteroids, is an environment highly rich in resources. Celestial bodies contain highly concentrated quantities of metals such as iron, nickel, tungsten cobalt, and Rare Earth elements, as well as gasses such as ammonia, nitrogen, and hydrogen.[13] Comets are mostly frozen water embedded with dust particles while rocky asteroids are composed of carbon-rich, metallic, and

9   Howell, Elizabeth. "Lagrange Points: Parking Places in Space," *Space.com*, August 21, 2017, available at <https://www.space.com/30302-lagrange-points.html>

10 Ibid.

11 Deudney, Daniel. *Dark Skies: Space Expansionism, Planetary Geopolitics, and the End of Humanity* (Oxford: UP, 2016), pp. 101–102.

12 Howell, "Lagrange Points: Parking Places in Space."

13 The Government of the Grand Duchy of Luxemburg. "Resources in Space," *Space Resources.lu*, available at <http://www.spaceresources.public.lu/en/about.html#>

mineral-rich silicate materials.[14] The mining of these resources hold critical potential for the sustenance of life both on Earth and in space. The European Space Agency, Japanese Aerospace Exploration Agency, NASA, CNSA, and the Indian Space Research Organization are actively developing probes and programs to utilize these precious resources.[15,16] Planetary Resources and Deep Space Industries are expecting to deliver water from asteroids and create in-space refueling economies in the next ten years.[17]

Orbital knowledge, access to resources and technological capacity to traverse constitute key elements of space development. Sensitivities of the space environment, however, pose limitations on the type of activities and number of actors that could be involved in this venture. While our understanding of the cosmic map is expanding at an unprecedented rate, our ability to control the forces that shape this geography is minimal. The unique assets of space geography provide extraordinary and unprecedented capabilities for governmental and military strategy, but the manifestation of geopolitical rivalries pose an imminent threat to all aspirations in effect. Similar to the development of naval and air power, space power is a turning point in passion, property, and politics. Humanity is taking eager steps into space—and is taking everything that is human with it—curiosity, innovation, politics, and errors.

---

14 Ibid.

15 The Government of the Grand Duchy of Luxemburg. "Resources in Space."

16 Foust, Jeff. "NASA Seeks Proposal for Space Resources Technologies," *Space News,* December 6, 2017, available at <http://spacenews.com/nasa-seeks-proposals-for-space-resources-technologies/>

17 Wall, Mike. "Asteroid Mining May Be a Reality by 2025," *Space.com,* August 11, 2015, accessible at <https://www.space.com/30213-asteroid-mining-planetary-resources-2025.html>

ii. The Challenges Ahead:

As of now, the United States Munitions List (USML) classifies all spacecraft as "defense articles," which strictly limits the transfer of space technologies and information to foreign entities.[18] In effect, this regulation isolates the United States from international cooperative development by effectively restraining American companies and technologies from participating in the global market. It speaks to the political outcomes of isolationist and defensive policy in a globalized economy. No other country has such a classification or restriction in regard to space activity. It is of crucial importance for states and companies to have access to the global market both for trade, transparency, and accountability purposes. The American Bar Association of the United States suggests that the moving of nonmilitary spacecraft off of the USML and onto the less restrictive Commercial Control List might prevail more competition and interaction among space actors.[19] Such a move, of course, begs another series of regulations on commercial space activity, as the Outer Space Treaty mandates that each country retains jurisdiction and control both of its governmental and nongovernmental spacecraft.[20] The U.S. government recently started addressing this issue: the House of Representatives approved legislation on April 24, 2018, to create a licensing scheme for "non-traditional" commercial space activities.[21]

---

18 State Department's Internal Traffic in Arms Regulations (ITAR) imposes this restriction.

19 Kleiman, Matthew J. "Space Law 101: An Introduction to Space Law," *American Bar Association Young Lawyers Division,* available at <https://www.americanbar.org/groups/young_lawyers/publications/the_101_201_practice_series/space_law_101_an_introduction_to_space_law.html>

20 United Nations Office for Outer Space Affairs. "Resolution Adopted by the General Assembly," December 19, 1966, available at <http://www.unoosa.org/oosa/en/ourwork/spacelaw/treaties/outerspacetreaty.html>

21 Foust, Jeff. "House Passes Commercial Space Regulatory Bill," *Space News,*

Chairman of the House Science Committee grieved how legal uncertainty has "cramped capital formation and innovation, and has driven American companies overseas" and announced that "The Space Commerce Act remedies this situation by establishing a new, novel legal and policy framework that unleashes American free enterprise and business, assures conformity with Outer Space Treaty obligations and guarantees that the U.S. will lead the world in commercial space activities throughout the 21st century."[22]

In retrospect, commercial space activity hints at new legal and political challenges. It is argued that some countries might seek to attract private space companies by maintaining a loose regulatory regime in which operating costs taxes, and labor and environmental laws are significantly more lenient.[23] Thus, states can enter strategic partnerships with private companies to carry out research, launches, payloads etc. that do not have to be classified to be kept in discretion. Unlike its Earth counterpart, such behavior poses an existential security threat in space. A senior executive from Boeing—NASA's prime contractor on the ISS—warns for the danger of jeopardizing future private sector participation by handing the lead to commercial entities too soon.[24] "[Government reliance on private agents like SpaceX] emphasizes the incompatibility of these large-scale, long-term expensive projects with the short-term thinking generally employed by the political class."[25] The

April 25, 2018, available at <http://spacenews.com/house-passes-commercial-space-regulatory-bill/>

22 Ibid.

23 Kleiman, "Space Law 101: An Introduction to Space Law."

24 Trump Budget Cuts U.S. Cash for International Space Station," *BBC*, February 12, 2018, available at <http://www.bbc.com/news/world-us-canada-43038329>

25 Clegg, Brian. *Final Frontier: The Pioneering Science and Technology of Explor-*

safe and secure development of space programs require utmost awareness of space actors and the space environment. It is essential to address the commercial issue before undermining international trust and overall security.

iii. Space Debris:

Underpinning the very foundation of space activity, the most immediate challenge to space development appears to be space debris.[26] Every launch into orbit creates debris—nonfunctional, human-made objects, including fragments and elements thereof, in Earth orbit or re-entering into Earth's atmosphere.[27] Given the magnitude of kinetic energy between space objects, it is theorized that impact collisions are increasingly more unavoidable. As the amount of debris in orbit heightens, the possibility of collision-born debris generation increases in a cascading phenomenon.[28,29] A cancerous growth in debris could potentially impede or inhibit the utilization of space for a modern civilization. In retrospect,

> the Chinese launch in 2007 increased the amount of debris in orbit below 2,000 km by one-fifth. The Russian Satellite Cosmos 2251's accidental collision with an American Iridium satellite in 2009 created over

---

ing the Universe. (New York, NY: St. Martin's Press, 2014), p. 169.

26 European Space Agency. "Space Debris: Frequently Asked Questions," January 24, 2018, available at <http://www.esa.int/Our_Activities/ Operations/Space_Debris/FAQ_Frequently_asked_questions>

27 " [...] from defunct or unused satellites, spent rocket stages, detached explosive couplings, a runaway toolkit, flecks of paint, and anything else that does not serve a human-derived purpose in orbit." Bowen, "Cascading Crises: Orbital Debris and the Widening of Space Security," p. 48.

28 Which is known as the "Kessler Syndrome."

29 Bowen, "Cascading Crises: Orbital Debris and the Widening of Space Security," p. 49.

1,200 pieces of tracked debris. The number of detected and tracked debris objects from these two debris events is over 5,500, and they make up 36% of all objects residing in or passing through the low Earth orbit—where most surveillance and observation satellites are positioned. These numbers only include the debris that can be tracked by space surveillance networks (SSN) as part of SSA efforts, which are usually greater than 10 cm in diameter.[30]

As of 2018, there are more than 42,000 tracked debris in the orbit, and 23,000 that remain in space are regularly tracked by the U.S. Space Surveillance Network.[31] Russia/Former USSR, United States and China are responsible for 16,565 major orbiting materials (from satellites to debris) out of 17,946.[32] Russia accounts for 3,961 detectable space debris, and the United States for 3,999. Being a new space power, China is already responsible for more than "2,300 trackable pieces of junk, more than 35,000 pieces larger than a thumbnail, and perhaps hundreds of thousands of pieces too small to track."[33] The increasing amount of space debris poses a serious threat to many spy and remote observation satellites that are placed in the low Earth orbit (LEO), where impact collisions are observed and expected. "Satellites and the International Space Station are routinely moved to avoid orbital debris, and occasionally the inhabitants of the ISS are required to take shelter in station's

---

30 Ibid.

31 European Space Agency. "Space Debris: About Space Debris," February 21, 2018, available at <https://www.esa.int/Our_Activities/Operations/Space_Debris/About_space_debris>

32 Mosher, D., & Kiersz, A. "These Are the Countries on Earth with the Most Junk in Space," *Business Insider*, October 20, 2017, available at <http://www.businessinsider.com/space-debris-garbage-statistics-country-list-2017-10>

33 Ibid.

lifeboat as a precautionary measure when an avoidance ma-
neuver is not possible."[34] It is of crucial importance, both for financial and security reasons, to stabilize the debris population
through a combination of strong adherence to existing mitigation guidelines and improved efforts to eliminate existing
debris. It is argued that even the active removal of at least five
objects per year that have relatively large mass and high probability of collision would make considerable impact.[35] This issue
further complicates space policy as opinions on how to classify
space debris vary.

iv. Addressing Space Debris:

The Outer Space Treaty's Article VI states that,

> States Parties to the Treaty shall bear international re-
> sponsibility for national activities in outer space, in-
> cluding the Moon and other celestial bodies, whether
> such activities are carried on by governmental agencies
> or by non-governmental entities, and for assuring that
> national activities are carried out in conformity with the
> provisions set forth in the present Treaty. The activities
> of non-governmental entities in outer space, including
> the Moon and other celestial bodies, shall require au-
> thorization and continuing supervision by the appro-
> priate State Party to the Treaty [emphasis added].[36]

---

34 Kleiman, "Space Law 101: An Introduction to Space Law."

35 Vedda, James. "Orbital Debris Remediation Through International Engagement," *Center for Space Policy and Strategy*, March 2017, available at <http://
www.aerospace.org/wp-content/uploads/2017/09/DebrisRemediation
.pdf>, p. 4.

36 United Nations Office for Outer Space Affairs. "United Nations Treaties
and Principles on Outer Space, Related General Assembly Resolutions and
Other Documents," available at <http://www.unoosa.org/pdf/publications
/ST_SPACE_061Rev01E.pdf>

The article imposes several obligations on states such as responsibility, transparency, accountability, and cooperation. Along with Article VI, Article VII helps identify liability for damage caused by objects in space. Article IX allows "states that have reason to believe that a planned activity or experiment would cause potentially harmful interference with other space activities to 'request consultation' concerning the activity or experiment."[37] The Liability Convention assesses damage in space by objects, but has a much more specific guideline to determine intentions before charging for damages or liability. Such an assessment requires information from the Registration Convention, which urges states to register their space activities to provide information on any objects launched and the objects' orbital parameters. It also directs nations with monitoring or tracking facilities to aid in the identification of space objects that caused damage.[38] These three articles and the given conventions address issues pertaining to space debris, and collectively acknowledge the critical role of debris mitigation. However, there are grey zones in the legislature that beg further attention for a safer space environment. For instance, the "consultations" suggested in Article IX do not necessarily offer remediation, but only offer guidance in future policy. Similarly, the Liability Convention falls short on meeting its goal of assigning costs, as there is no "ownership" of space debris. Given the ambiguity in international treaties, interested parties have proposed the adoption of voluntary "rules of the road" to guide behaviors in space as an alternative to the long and delicate process of creating a legally binding treaty. While

---

37 National Research Council. *Orbital Debris: A Technical Assessment* (Washington, DC: The National Academies Press 1995), available at <https://www.nap.edu/read/4765/chapter/14#186>, p. 186.

38 Ibid.

not consolidating remediation efforts, this alternative helps with orbital debris mitigation.[39]

Undeniably, there are formidable technical challenges involving the testing and deployment of remediation systems: mainly, the double-use function of ASAT systems. "Any system that can conduct tracking, rendezvous, and manipulation of a satellite can destroy it or at least disrupt its functions."[40] The 2007 Chinese and 2008 American tests illustrated both the perceived threats and international distrust that pose a grave obstruction to possible remedial operations. Yet, despite the discursive and contextual problems, it is clear that the international community is increasingly more aware of the need for clarity and uniformity in legislation for a safer operational domain. Today, both NASA and CNSA adhere to the Inter-Agency Space Debris Coordination Committee's (IADC) mitigation guidelines in their conduct and actively participate in cooperative efforts.[41]

v. A Greater Threat—Nuclear Proliferation:

Space debris is perhaps the most immediate challenge pertaining to the utilization of space. However, it only preludes a greater challenge: variations in utilization. A stabilized space prevails a dual-use dilemma in which space technology could be used both to improve developmental services and to advance weapons systems. Some of the existing counterspace weapons are kinetic physical weapons that attempt to strike

---

39 Vedda, "Orbital Debris Remediation Through International Engagement," p. 4.

40 Ibid.

41 United Nations Office for Outer Space Affairs, Inter-Agency Space Debris Coordination Committee. "IACD Space Guidelines," September 2007, available at <http://www.unoosa.org/documents/pdf/spacelaw/sd/IADC-2002-01-IADC-Space_Debris-Guidelines-Revision1.pdf>

directly or detonate a warhead near satellite or ground operation, non-kinetic physical weapons including lasers, high-pow-
ered microwaves and electromagnetic pulse weapons that have
physical effects on space systems without making physical
contact, electronic attacks that target the means by which
space systems transmit and receive data by jamming or spoof-
ing radiofrequency signals, and cyberattacks that target data
itself and the systems that use this data.[42] The United States
holds superiority in all of these aforementioned technologies,
and China has develop capacity in all but non-kinetic physical
weapons.[43] While space-based military support missions already enhance the capacities of land, air, and sea forces to accu-
rately engage and destroy targets worldwide,[44] the possibility
of space-based nuclear weapons offers a game-changing effect.
There is widespread concern over intentions and ambitions on
both the Chinese and American sides. However, as of now, nuclear energy is used only to power exploration missions. Voy-
agers 1 and 2, the Apollo Lunar Surface Experiments Packages,
and the Curiosity rover were powered by radioisotope ther-
moelectric generators (RTGs), and SNAP-10A was powered
by a nuclear power plant hosted in its body.[45] While the Spirit
and Opportunity rovers, the Phoenix lander and the Curiosity
rover all used power systems with less than 200 Watts, manned
missions to Mars will likely require systems with 40,000 to
50,000 Watts—effectively necessitating more advanced nu-

42 Harrison, T., Johnson, K., & Roberts, T.G. *Space Threat Assessment 2018*
    (Washington, DC: Center for Strategic and International Studies, 2018),
    available at <https://aerospace.csis.org/spacethreat2018/>

43 Ibid.

44 Dolman, *Astropolitik: Classical Geopolitics in the Space Age*, p. 26.

45 Tasoff, Harrison. "Kilopower Project: NASA Pushes Nuclear Power for
    Deep-Space Missions," *Space.com*, January 22, 2018, available at <https://
    www.scientificamerican.com/article/nasa-pushes-for-nuclear-powered-
    space-missions/>

clear reactors.[46] Currently, NASA is working on the Kilopower reactor which uses active nuclear fission to harvest energy from uranium. Successful Kilopower reactors are projected to be installed in the lunar orbit, on the moon's surface and in Mars missions.[47] Nuclear power is undeniably essential for space exploration and utilization, but its potentially offensive use and propensity for accidents raise anxieties. The strategic advantages of space-based nuclear capacity are incomparable to any other strategic advantage ever known to military bodies. However, the scientific miscalculations and political assumptions that characterize humanity's presence in space thus-far necessitate nuclear proliferation to be seen as more of an imminent danger than a strategic advantage. Space environment poses certain challenges that are yet to be overcome. Extreme temperatures, intense fluxes of radiation, absence of physical matter and weight, along with the very orbits, velocity, and gravity wells of the Earth predicate great caution in deploying the most destructive war instrument humans have ever created into the most sensitive environment they have ever been to.

As the Chinese–American discourse illustrates, foreign policy decisions are influenced by a variety of factors that do not necessarily benefit the security interests of state actors. Along with mirroring behavior, power maximization, utility maximiza-tion, and the construction of normative worlds, human psychology, and individual-level empirical assumptions imprint onto state behavior as cognitive errors, misperceptions, and biases of individuals or groups.[48] For instance, force de-

---

46 Ibid.

47 Ibid.

48 Erisen, Elif. "An Introduction to Political Psychology for International Relations Scholars," *Center for Strategic Research*, 2012, available at <https://pdfs.semanticscholar.org/49f7/0a376d3ac742045afbf1c38a30dd085844dc.pdf>

ployments are sometimes a response to strong domestic political pressures to increase military budgets, develop and exploit new weapon technologies, or deploy weapon systems simply because an adversary is doing so.[49] Moreover, images or stereotypes of foreign nations play a determining role in the making of foreign policy. Given these images and stereotypes, low probability events gain overwhelming subjective weight in policy discussions in the face of perceived risks.[50] Several factors are found to inform political decision-making processes: (i) political attitudes that are learnt from social context, which later manifest as strong social cognitive and emotional mechanisms that operate between leadership and the public,[51] (ii) presentation and evaluation methods that pertain to policy-proposals that involve certain biases which reduce outcomes to simple gains and losses relative to a status-quo reference point,[52] (iii) political ideology and regime struggles. Roosevelt's behavior in the Munich crisis, the U-2 crisis, the Suez crisis, the Iranian hostage rescue mission, and many other crisis situations that have been studied affirm the informants of decision-making under conditions of perceived risks.[53] There are numerous factors that contribute to defects in foreign policy decisions, and the antagonistic nature of international relations in space calls for a reassessment of strategic deterrence systems. Space is a particularly strategic and sensitive geography which necessitates sound decision-making.

---

49 U.S. Congress, Office of Technology Assessment, *Ballistic Missile Defense Technologies* (Washington, DC: U.S. Government Printing Office, September 1985), available at <https://www.princeton.edu/~ota/disk2/1985/8504/850408.PDF>, p. 121.

50 Erisen, "An Introduction to Political Psychology for International Relations Scholars," p. 21.

51 Ibid., p. 18.

52 Ibid., p. 12.

53 Ibid., p. 20.

The ultimate goal of the development and deployment of U.S. weapons systems is to reduce offenses by increasing defenses.[54] Complications with perceived incentives and disincentives in the Cold War era, however, demonstrate the challenges with theories of stability and assured deterrence. Decisions to develop or use nuclear weapons are informed by a plethora of factors ranging from the circumstances leading up to the crisis, the personal attributes of the leaders, their perception of each country's military capabilities and vulnerabilities, their perception of their adversary's incentives and intentions, to the doctrines of the two countries regarding nuclear strategy.[55] The variety and subjectivity of factors that shape the formation of nuclear policy, in force, make it highly defective. For the political means and ends concerned, nuclear policy in space is very similar to its Earth-based counterpart. While having a different outlook, the North Korea–U.S. nuclear crisis of 2017–18, for instance, illustrated a very similar problem to the Cold War— yet to affirm one thing: nuclear capacity is perceived as a tool for diplomatic leverage and as a guarantor of security interests. The fear of being pre-empted still pressures states to weigh the risks of striking first instead of waiting to be struck. However, the world is much different than that during the Cold War. Along with expanding levels of economic interdependence, the environmental peculiarities of space impose new restrictions and considerations that redefine what nuclear weaponization means for defense strategy.

There are two main strategic goals of demonstrated nuclear capacity: crisis stability and arms race stability. Crisis stability refers to the degree to which strategic force characteristics might, in a crisis situation, reduce incentives to initiate

---

54 U.S. Congress, Office of Technology Assessment, *Ballistic Missile Defense Technologies,* p. 133.

55 Ibid., p. 119.

the use of nuclear weapons.[56] In space, nuclear attacks offer (with the assumption of full control) outstanding precision and magnitude of destruction—making space-based weaponry the ultimate deterrent. However, there are several issues with that. First of all, threat avoidance is a very complicated problem, and debris interference endangers all orbiting objects and their missions. For example, even if there is absolute control over the spacecraft and the weapons involved, environmental hazards such as untracked debris between the weapon and the object of interest could result with a failure of mission. Secondly, objects in the orbit may slip from their trajectory. A "slip," meaning a lack focus and loose technical criteria for accurate inclusion systems for near-term missile deployments, leads to lack of full control over the orbiting object.[57] The assistant secretary and the former director of operational tests and evaluation at DoD stated in his 2002 review of the status of the missile defense programs, that "all U.S. missile defense programs—both theater and national—have slipped."[58] Similarly, the 2005 testing of the Demonstration of Autonomous Randezvous Technology (DART), a potentially dual-use satellite inspection system, ended with its range-finding system malfunctioning, slipping and causing an embarrassing collision with the target satellite.[59] Orbital slipping poses severe calculation complications on security operations that are potentially self-destructive—both to the weapons and actors involved. Lastly, the dual-use function of ADRs (as ASAT) pose a demonstrated existential threat to all orbiting objects—which brings into question any ra-

56 Ibid.

57 Moltz, *The Politics of Space Security*, p. 273.

58 Coyle, Philip. "Rhetoric or Reality? Missile Defense Under Bush," *Arms Control Association*, May 1, 2002, available at<https://www.armscontrol.org/act/2002_05/coylemay02>

59 Moltz, *The Politics of Space Security*, p. 293.

tionale for positioning such valuable and expensive[60] assets at an exceptionally vulnerable situation. ASAT systems create a crisis stability situation for all parties with the same capacity that have about the same losses at stake. "Space-based weapons cannot protect satellites, as these weapons are vulnerable to the same types of attack as the objects they are meant to protect."[61] Moreover, even the destructive use of ADR systems on technologically incompetent adversaries is likely to prove unfavorable, as increased debris population risks the safe use of space for all parties. It could be argued that space-based nuclear weapons don't provide enough incentives for states to invest in. In effect, these threats create a revised "crisis stability" in which incentives to initiate the use of nuclear weapons are reduced for all parties involved. Any of these three scenarios that involve nuclear capacity contain a grim probability of casting apocalypse on Earth. The losses associated with nuclear aggression or accidents in space catalyze a redefinition of crisis stability in which stability depends on the nonexistence of nuclear power.

Arms race stability concerns the effect of planned deployments on the scope and pace of the arms race to disincentivize the buildup of a nuclear force.[62] Demonstrations of perceived military or strategic superiority in space, especially in the Chinese–American discourse, carry the great risk of escalating to a classical security dilemma in which existential mantras justify defensive actions that result in self-fulfilling prophecies of aggression.[63] Given the sensitivities of the space environment,

---

60 For more information on the cost of space launches, visit: Kramer, S., & Mosher, D. "Here's how Much Money It Actually Costs to Launch Stuff into Space," *Business Insider,* July 20, 2016, available at <http://www.businessinsider.com/spacex-rocket-cargo-price-by-weight-2016-6>

61 Podvig, "Russian and Chinese Responses to U.S. Military Plans in Space."

62 U.S. Congress, Office of Technology Assessment, *Ballistic Missile Defense Technologies,* p. 119.

63 Boulegue, Mathieu. "The Russia-NATO Relationship Between a Rock and

such a display of power risks more than it could possibly offer. As the development of war technologies (nuclear, informational, cyber, space, et cetera) illustrate, technologic advancement is not unique to any state or nation, and is only an advantage for so long. Scientific breakthrough leads to the proliferation of counter-technologies which ironically increases both the ways and means of making war in an effort to limit the occurrence or destruction of war.[64] Science, due to its instrumental nature, is always inferior to politics, and thus is incapable of solving the conundrum of war. It offers solutions to the problems of war in war,[65] that serve to those who use its methods.[66] Militarized science prompts the development of offensive weaponry,[67] triggering a vicious circle of war and scientific discovery that fulfill each other's needs. "Science cannot abolish war because science has become war, and war become science," writes the Air University's first space theorist Everett Dolman.[68] The internal and external factors that shape the Chinese and American nuclear force postures have been costly, indecisive, and "destabilizing." Arms race stability in space is a very improbable policy option with many fatal consequences attached. "Nuclear strategy must be assessed along other axes—deterrence effectiveness, cost effectiveness, bureaucratic feasibility, domestic politics, and alliance politics to name but five—and we should certainly not assume a priori that the policy that maximizes strategic stability will simultaneously maximize all

---

a Hard Place: How the 'Defensive Inferiority Syndrome' Is Increasing the Potential for Error," *The Journal of Slavic Military Studies 30/3*, July 25, 2017, available at <https://www.tandfonline.com/doi/pdf/10.1080/13518046.2017.1341769?needAccess=true>

64 Dolman, *Can Science End War?*, p. 4.

65 Ibid., p. 12.

66 Ibid, p. 6.

67 Ibid., p. 34.

68 Dolman, *Astropolitik: Classical Geopolitics in the Space Age*, p. 168.

of the other variables. Crafting the optimal nuclear strategy almost certainly involves trade-offs and it is by defining strategic stability most narrowly that we are most likely to set up a sensible debate about what those trade-offs should be."[69] Successful strategic stability relies on a clear understanding of the actions and actors that are to be deterred. It is unclear—and increasingly contested—that the possession of nuclear weapons actually deters adversaries from the buildup of nuclear capacity. It is unclear what such capacity aims to deter, too. In retrospect, it is widely argued that Russian motives were misunderstood during the Cold War. The contemporary Iranian and North Korean nuclear development speaks to developmental goals as much as they do to security concerns. North Korea, for instance, just announced the initiation of "complete denuclearization" and peace talks with South Korea after on April 2018, upon declaring its completion of nuclear experimentation.[70] "No plan survives contact with the enemy," wrote von Moltke more than a century ago. Today, it is essential to remember that plans, no matter if informed by algorithms or satellite data, are still developed against a set of assumptions and beliefs on the adversaries' capacity and intentions. However, history shows that an active opponent in the field is as intelligent and motivated as the attacker. [71] A perceived military superiority is

69 Acton, James. "Reclaiming Strategic Stability," *Carnegie Endowment for International Peace Strategic Studies Institute,* February 5, 2013, available at <http://carnegieendowment.org/2013/02/05/reclaiming-strategic-stability-pub-51032>

70 Kim, C., Smith, J., & Rampton, R. "Korean Leaders Set 'Denuclearization' Goal, Trump Says Will Maintain Pressure," *Reuters,* April 26, 2018, available at <https://www.reuters.com/article/us-northkorea-southkorea/korean-leaders-aim-for-end-of-war-complete-denuclearisation-after-historic-summit-idUSKBN1HX2I>

71 Weeden, Brian. "Space Weaponization: Aye or Nay?" *Arms Control Today,* November 4, 2008, available at <https://www.armscontrol.org/act/2008_11/Book_review>

unlikely to generate an insurmountable strategic advantage to any state, but might spur other states and actors to find ways to counter such weapons or avoid their effects.[72] "The debate over space weaponization should come down to three things: security, safety, and sustainability. Whatever the answer is, it should properly address all three of those elements. Space weapons, however defined, may serve some space security needs. If that comes at the cost of a reduction in the other two factors, clearly it is not a viable option. Likewise, certain proposals that have been made for international regimes and bans on weapons may in theory create safety, but if they ignore the security concerns of space-faring nations, they will ultimately be counterproductive. Only by factoring in all three considerations and working together can the world move forward with utilization of space for the peaceful benefit of all states."[73] Strategic stability in space could only be built upon a nuanced understanding of interdependence and shared vulnerabilities.

vi. Addressing Strategic Stability and Arms Control:

The space domain lacks an updated and comprehensive legislature for states to adhere to. The only international legal framework for space conduct remains the Outer Space Treaty of 1967, which accounts only states as responsible actors. It defines space as "a common heritage of humankind, and an area for peaceful exploitation."[74] While prohibiting the placement of weapons of mass destruction in orbit and usage of the moon or other celestial bodies for military purposes, it

---

72 Ibid.

73 Ibid.

74 Meyer, Paul. "U.S. Space Security Policy: Still in Orbit or Commencing Re-entry?" *Centre for International Policy Studies, University of Ottawa 10* (October 2010), available at <http://www.cips-cepi.ca/wp-content/uploads/2015/01/Meyer_PB_3.pdf>, p. 2.

permits military operations as long as they correspond to the "peaceful purposes" provision.[75] By leaving a huge grey zone for space actors to undertake questionable actions, this clause undermines states' ability to place and operate assets outside the Earth's atmosphere without external interference, damage, or destruction.[76] In effect, the Outer Space Treaty (OST) addresses the needs of the Cold War, and is incompatible with modern technology and contemporary politics. Establishment of international law and regulations governing space activity is the first step to providing a safe operational ground both for state and commercial actors. The Space Law Committee of the International Law Association, Inter-Agency Space Debris Coordination Committee (in coordination with the ESA, Russian Space Agency, NASA and Jaxa), International Astronautical Academy, and International Institute of Space Law are some of the international bodies working to codify a legal framework for debris management and mitigation.[77] The Nuclear Suppliers Group, the Missile Technology Control Regime, the Hague Code of Conduct against Ballistic missile Proliferation, and the Wassenaar Agreement are some of the bilateral and plurilateral treaties that seek to reduce or eliminate certain categories of nuclear weapons.[78] The Treaty on the Non-Proliferation of Nuclear Weapons, the Partial Test Ban Treaty (PTBT), and the Comprehensive Nuclear-Test-Ban Treaty are waiting to enter into force since 1996.[79] There are numerous treaties and organizations working to codify law and regulations to make space a safer place,

---

75 Ibid.

76 Moltz, *The Politics of Space Security,* p. 11.

77 National Research Council, *Orbital Debris: A Technical Assessment,* pp. 187–188.

78 United Nations Office for Disarmament Affairs. "Nuclear Weapons," available at <https://www.un.org/disarmament/wmd/nuclear/>

79 Ibid.

but the question is whether they can catch up with the pace of technological development.[80]

---

80 To see the full literature on International Arms Control, visit: Georgetown Law Library, "International Arms Control Research Guide," available at <http://guides.ll.georgetown.edu/c.php?g=363499&p=2455907>

V. CONCLUSION:

We set sail on this new sea because there is new knowledge to be gained and new rights to be won, and they must be won and used for the progress of all people. For space science, like nuclear science and all technology, has no conscience of its own. Whether it will become a force for good or ill depends on man, and only if the United States occupies a position of pre-eminence can we help decide whether this new ocean will be a sea of peace or a new terrifying theater of war.

John F. Kennedy

Reaching for the skies has had a spiritual connotation throughout human history. From the ancient Egyptians to the Mayans, the Romans to the Chinese, understandings of the universe have shaped human civilizations, social and political institutions. The first lunar landings were seen to be "equal in importance to that moment in evolution when aquatic life came crawling up on the land."[1] The ability to complete successful launches, send satellites into orbit and ultimately living beings into space has corresponded not only to curiosity, but also to a desire to assert ideological superiority, restore national pride, and assert international political power. The broad narrative of space expansionism is increasingly so a form of science-based and technology-dependent religion that advances itself as the extrapolation and culmination of the biological evolution of life on Earth and the cosmos.[2] At a critical juncture in human history, as Mars exploration and

---

1   Braun, as quoted by Deudney, *Dark Skies: Space Expansionism, Planetary Geopolitics, and the End of Humanity,* p. 22.

2   Deudney, *Dark Skies: Space Expansionism, Planetary Geopolitics, and the End of Humanity,* pp. 34–37.

colonization is the beginning of a greater expansion, it is of crucial importance to be aware of the ideological, psychological, and political factors that influence policy in a field-like space that corresponds to the ethos of many civilizations, past and present. The Chinese–American discourse illustrates precisely the interplay of these factors, to signal that space policy is a form of foreign policy, and foreign policy decisions are not necessarily rational.

There is a revolving debate among scholars on how to proceed with space development. Moltz breaks down the two conflicting schools as "space defense" and "space sanctuary."[3] "Space defense" encompasses ideas of *space nationalism and technological determinism*—which is grounded in the ideas of Thucydides, Machiavelli, and Hobbes. This school of thinking anticipates an inherent state of war, mitigated through *realpolitik*. Views of critical names such as Everett C. Dolman of the U.S. Air Force's School of Advanced Air Power Studies, or Joan Johnson-Freese of the Naval War College are some of the examples of this school of thinking. "Space sanctuary," on the other hand, encompasses *global interactionism and social interactionism*—which mainly grounds in Kantian ideas of universalist thinking. Views of the Air Force Lieutenant Colonel Bruce DeBlois or Congressman Dennis Kucinich are examples of this school of thinking. As much as worldwide national policies follow the first stream of thinking, international conventions and treaties serve to the second one—sending waves of relief to peace-seekers of future in space. Given the known and predicted challenges of space development, it is wise "to take the referent object in space security as the space environment itself."[4] In the infinite vastness of astronomically

---

3   Moltz, *The Politics of Space Security,* p. 23.

4   Bowen, "Cascading Crises: Orbital Debris and the Widening of Space Security," p. 53.

destructive forces, employment of national securitization measures is counterproductive to security interests. Instead, international cooperation with a shared informational basis could help the realization of the space quest. However, it is questionable that the predominant political doctrines and practices will immediately adjust to the reality of this unforgiving environment. Successful introduction of interdependent progress in space goes hand-in-hand with its successful introduction into existing earth politics.[5]

The Chinese–American discourse highlights critical discursive issues pertaining to policy-making. The cascade of events between China and the United States seem to be creating a self-fulfilling prophecy of the American military's propensity to view China as the "enemy,"[6] while the nature of Chinese growth continues to provoke U.S. national security "insecurities." Efforts to remedy relations do not seem to constitute a major turning point in this discourse as term dependent decisions, impulsive reactions and immediate political gains risk eternal damages. Interpretive differences and historical distrust in long-term intentions vehemently establish an aggressive space order, endangering services and technologies that are central to the geopolitical imperatives of each party. Some American strategists argue that "Freedom of action in space is essential not only to the American way of war but to the American way of life."[7] We are left to see how long the American and Chinese "ways of life" can coexist peacefully in the space domain, as well as on Earth. The longevity of peace-

---

5   Ibid., p. 16.

6   Oh, "Assessing Chinese Intentions for the Military Use of the Space Domain," p. 97.

7   Stalcup, Travis C. "U.S. in Space: Superiority, Not Dominance," *The Diplomat*, January 16, 2014, available at <https://thediplomat.com/2014/01/u-s-in-space-superiority-not-dominance/>

ful existence will remain a question in the face of recurrent and rising hostility as long as space conduct is perceived "in the context of general military operations."[8]

It is clear that both China and the U.S. recognize the importance of international cooperation for a sustainable future in space. However, their contrasting assessments of strategic deterrence—manifesting as increased militarization—undermine diplomatic efforts and trust-building practices. To reconcile this knowledge with the nuances of Chinese and American policies, it is important to understand the context and history of this relationship. It is important to understand that everything is done in the name of security. It is important to understand that, in space, security for one means security for everyone. Security is a concept much more widely construed that simple military capacity. The creation of a safer space necessitates the abandonment of mantras of dominance, superiority, and leadership. Although it may seem a compromise to those familiar with the aforementioned conventional security, cooperation doesn't have to mean a compromise of security interest. It is essential to understand that adversaries might not share the same notion of strategic stability, and the norms of armament might diverge. Given the rapid pace of technological advancement, nongovernmental activity, and environmental limitations, our understanding of space conduct is outdated. As the world economy increasingly relies on the use of space, revising the existing international legal framework for space conduct becomes more and more essential. Space development offers a new era; a window for humanity to reevaluate its priorities and needs in the face of startling transformations. "The most important practical discovery of the 'space age' has been an improved understanding of the

8   Moltz, *The Politics of Space Security,* p. 25.

Earth."[9] Space development is a unique chance for humanity to reassess power structures and political norms as "much of the actual agendas of movements for peace, arms control, and sustainability are essentially about alternative ways of ordering the material world and our relations with it."[10] Space technology, if effectively guided, could lead to a post-scarcity world where abundance is the norm, where there is less poverty and less conflict. It is time we determine what we want from ourselves and from the future.

---

9   Schouten, P. "Theory Talk #60: Daniel Deudney on Mixed Ontology, Planetary Geopolitics, and Republican Greenpeace," *Theory Talks*, November 20, 2013, available at <http://www.theorytalks.org/2013/11/theory-talk -60_285.html>, p. 13.

10 Ibid., p. 3.

VI. BIBLIOGRAPHY:

Acton, James. "Reclaiming Strategic Stability," *Carnegie Endowment for International Peace Strategic Studies Institute,* February 5, 2013, available at <http://carnegieendowment.org/2013/02/05/reclaiming-strategic-stability-pub-51032>

Al-Ekabi, C., & Ferretti, S. (Eds.), *Yearbook on Space Policy 2016: Space for Sustainable Development* (Springer International Publishing, 2018), p. 84.

Amadeo, Kimberly. "NASA Budget, Current Funding, and History," *The Balance,* March 24, 2018, available at <https://www.thebalance.com/nasa-budget-current-funding-and-history-3306321>

Baiocchi, D., & Welser, W. "The Democratization of Space: New Actors Need New Rules," *Foreign Affairs, 94*(3), 2015, 98–104, available at <https://www.foreignaffairs.com/articles/space/2015-04-20/democratization-space>

Blount, P.J. & Gabrynowicz, J.I. (Eds). "USA-193: Selected Documents," *Serial Topics in Aerospace Law Series 1* (2008), available at <http://www.spacelaw.olemiss.edu/resources/pdfs/usa193-selected-documents.pdf>

Boulegue, Mathieu. "The Russia-NATO Relationship Between a Rock and a Hard Place: How the 'Defensive Inferiority Syndrome' Is Increasing the Potential for Error," *The Journal of Slavic Military Studies 30/3,* July 25, 2017, available at <https://www.tandfonline.com/doi/df/10.1080/13518046.2017.1341769?needAccess=true>

Bowen, B.E. "Cascading Crises: Orbital Debris and the Widening of Space Security," *Astropolitics 12/1* (March

2014), available at <https://www.tandfonline.com/doi/fu ll/10.1080/14777622.2014.890489>

Broadway, Chuck. "STRATCOM Commander Offers Testimony—U.S. Armed Forces Ready to Deter Adversaries," *Milsat Magazine* (April 2018)

Central Committee of the Communist Party of China, "The 13th Five-Year Plan for Economic and Social Development of the People's Republic of China (2016–2020)," March 2016, available at <http://en.ndrc.gov.cn/newsrelease /201612/P020161207645765233498.pdf>

Clegg, Brian. *Final Frontier: The Pioneering Science and Technology of Exploring the Universe* (New York, NY: St. Martin's Press, 2014)

Cowen-Hirsh, Rebecca. "Leadership and Industry Development Pave a New Path for Unified SATCOM," *Milsat Magazine* (April 2018)

Coyle, Philip. "Rhetoric or Reality? Missile Defense Under Bush," *Arms Control Association*, May 1, 2002, available at<https://www.armscontrol.org/act/2002_05/coyle may02>

David, Leonard. "China to Launch Mars Rover in 2020," *Space. com,* April 27, 2016, available at <https://www.space. com/32715-china-mars-moon-exploration-plans.html>

"Decaying Spy Satellite USA 193," *Heavens Above,* available at <http://www.heavens-above.com/usa193.aspx>

Department of Defense of the United States of America, "National Security Space Strategy Unclassified Summary," January 2011, available at <https://www.dni.gov/files/

documents/Newsroom/Reports%20and%20Pubs/2011_ nationalsecurityspacestrategy.pdf>

Deudney, Daniel. *Dark Skies: Space Expansionism, Planetary Geopolitics, and the End of Humanity* (Oxford: UP, 2016)

Dolman, Everett Carl. *Can Science End War?* (Malden, MA: Polity Press, 2016)

Dolman, Everett Carl. *Astropolitik: Classical Geopolitics in the Space Age* (Portland, OR: Frank Cass Publishers, 2002)

Erisen, Elif. "An Introduction to Political Psychology for International Relations Scholars," *Center for Strategic Research*, 2012, available at <https://pdfs.semanticscholar. org/49f7/0a376d3ac742045afbf1c38a30dd085844dc. pdf>

Erwin, Sandra. "Military Leaders: National Security Space Shown the Love," April 17, 2018, available at <http:// spacenews.com/military-leaders-national-security- space-shown-the-love/>

European Space Agency. "Space Debris: Frequently Asked Questions," January 24, 2018, available at <http://www. esa.int/Our_Activities/Operations/Space_Debris/FAQ_ Frequently_asked_questions>

"Exclusive: Putin Blames U.S. for Arms Race, Denies 'New Cold War'," *NBC News*, March 1, 2018, available at <https:// www.nbcnews.com/nightly-news/video/exclusive-putin- denies-cold-war-1174558275948>

Foust, Jeff. "House Passes Commercial Space Regulatory Bill," *Space News*, April 25, 2018, available at <http://spacenews. com/house-passes-commercial-space-regulatory-bill/>

Foust, Jeff. "NASA Seeks Proposal for Space Resources Technologies," *Space News*, December 6, 2017, available at <http://spacenews.com/nasa-seeks-proposals-for-space-resources-technologies/>

Foust, Jeff. "New National Space Strategy Emphasizes 'America First' Policies," *Space News*, March 24, 2018, available at <https://spacenews.com/new-national-space-strategy-emphasizes-america-first-policies/>

Foust, Jeff. "U.S. Dismisses Space Weapons Treaty Proposal as 'Fundamentally Flawed'," *Space News*, September 11, 2014, available at <http://spacenews.com/41842us-dismisses-space-weapons-treaty-proposal-as-fundamentally-flawed/>

Georgetown Law Library, "International Arms Control Research Guide," available at <http://guides.ll.georgetown.edu/c.php?g=363499&p=2455907>

Grondin, David. *Securing Outer Space*. Ed. Natalie Bormann (London: Routledge, 2009)

Howell, Elizabeth. "China National Space Administration: Facts & Information," *Space.com*, May 25, 2016, available at <https://www.space.com/22743-china-national-space-administration.html>

Hodge, N., Starr, B., Chance, M., & Burrows, Emma. "Putin Claims New 'Invincible' Missile Can Pierce US Defenses," *CNN*, March 1, 2018, available at <https://edition.cnn.com/2018/03/01/europe/putin-russia-missile-intl/>

Howell, Elizabeth. "Lagrange Points: Parking Places in Space," *Space.com*, August 21, 2017, available at <https://www.space.com/30302-lagrange-points.html>

Huang, Echo. "China's Fallen Space Lab Was a Prism for Its Space Ambitions," *Quartz,* March 26, 2018, available at <https://qz.com/1232198/tiangong-1-chinas-falling-space-lab-is-a-prism-for-its-space-ambitions/?utm_source=atlfb>

Harrison, T., Johnson, K., & Roberts, T.G. *Space Threat Assessment 2018* (Washington, DC: Center for Strategic and International Studies, 2018), available at <https://aerospace.csis.org/spacethreat2018/>

Kakaes, K. "Weapons in Space," *CQ Global Researcher*, Issue 5, August 16, 2011, available at <http://library.cqpress.com/cqresearcher/document.php?id=cqrglobal2011081600>

Kim, C., Smith, J., & Rampton, R. "Korean Leaders Set 'Denuclearization' Goal, Trump Says Will Maintain Pressure," *Reuters*, April 26, 2018, available at <https://www.reuters.com/article/us-northkorea-southkorea/korean-leaders-aim-for-end-of-war-complete-denuclearisation-after-historic-summit-idUSKBN1HX2I>

Kleiman, Matthew J. "Space Law 101: An Introduction to Space Law," *American Bar Association Young Lawyers Division,* 2013, available at <https://www.americanbar.org/groups/young_lawyers/publications/the_101_201_practice_series/space_law_101_an_introduction_to_space_law.html>

Kramer, S., & Mosher, D. "Here's How Much Money It Actually Costs to Launch Stuff into Space," *Business Insider,* July 20, 2016, available at <http://www.businessinsider.com/spacex-rocket-cargo-price-by-weight-2016-6>

Mastalir, A.J. *The US Response to China's ASAT Test: An International Security Space Alliance for the Future* (Montgomery, AL: Air University Press, 2009), available at <www.jstor.org/stable/resrep13986>

Meyer, Paul. "U.S. Space Security Policy: Still in Orbit or Commencing Re-entry?" *Centre for International Policy Studies, University of Ottawa 10* (October 2010), available at <http://www.cips-cepi.ca/wp-content/uploads/2015/01/Meyer_PB_3.pdf>

Merian, 1st Lt. Christopher. "AFSPC Commander Unveils Three Major Space Initiatives at 33rd Space Symposium," *Headquarters Air Force Space Command Public Affairs*, April 7, 2017, available at <http://www.afspc.af.mil/News/Article-Display/Article/1145448/afspc-commander-unveils-three-major-space-initiatives-at-33rd-space-symposium/>

Ministry of National Defense of the People's Republic of China, "China's Military Strategy," May 26, 2015, available at <http://eng.mod.gov.cn/Press/2015-05/26/content_4586805_6.htm>

Moltz, J.C. *The Politics of Space Security: Strategic Restraint and the Pursuit of National Interests* (Stanford, CA: Stanford University Press, 2011)

National Aeronautics and Space Administration (NASA). "Aeronautics and Space Report of the President, Fiscal Year 2016 Activities," June 12, 2017, available at <https://history.nasa.gov/presrep2016.pdf>

National Research Council. *Orbital Debris: A Technical Assessment* (Washington, DC: The National Academies Press 1995), available at <https://www.nap.edu/read/4765/chapter/14#186>

Oh, Paul. "Assessing Chinese Intentions for the Military Use of the Space Domain," *Joint Forces Quarterly*, Issue 64, 1st Quarter, January 2012, <http://www.dtic.mil/dtic/tr/fulltext/u2/a575520.pdf>

People's Liberation Army. "China's Military Strategy," *China Military Online*, May 26, 2015, available at <http://english.chinamil.com.cn/news-channels/2015-05/26/content_6507716_2.htm>

Podvig, Pavel, & Hui, Zhang. "Russian and Chinese Responses to U.S. Military Plans in Space, Chapter 2." *American Academy of Arts & Sciences*, March 2008, available at <https://www.amacad.org/content/publications/pubContent.aspx?d=1201>

President of Russia. "Presidential Address to the Federal Assembly," March 1, 2018, available at <http://en.kremlin.ru/events/president/news/56957>

Rosenthal, E., & Sanger, D.E. "U.S. Plane in China After It Collides with Chinese Jet," *The New York Times,* April 2, 2001, available at <https://www.nytimes.com/2001/04/02/world/us-plane-in-china-after-it-collides-with-chinese-jet.html>

"Russia Proposes Space Weapons Ban," *Al-Jazeera*, February 12, 2008, available at <https://www.aljazeera.com/news/europe/2008/02/2008525132324551376.html>

Schouten, P. "Theory Talk #60: Daniel Deudney on Mixed Ontology, Planetary Geopolitics, and Republican Greenpeace," *Theory Talks*, November 20, 2013, available at <http://www.theorytalks.org/2013/11/theory-talk-60_285.html>

Schrogl, K., Blandina, B., Christophe, V., & Wolfgang, R. (Eds.).

Yearbook on Space Policy 2008/2009: Setting New Trends (Vienna: Springer-Verlag Wien, 2010).

Space Policy Online. "Military/National Security Space Activities," March 2018, available at <https://spacepolicyonline.com/topics/militarynational-security-space-activities/#policy1>

Sponable, Jess. "A Boost for Military Spaceplanes," *Aerospace America* 56/4 (April 2018)

Stone, C. "The Implications of Chinese Strategic Culture and Counter-Intervention upon Department of Defense Space Deterrence Operations," *Comparative Strategy*, December 7, 2016, <https://doi.org/10.1080/01495933.2016.1240964>

Stalcup, Travis C. "U.S. in Space: Superiority, Not Dominance," *The Diplomat*, January 16, 2014, available at <https://thediplomat.com/2014/01/u-s-in-space-superiority-not-dominance/>

Svitak, Amy. "Bolden Details Trip to China During Marshall Visit," *Space News*, November 19, 2010, available at <http://spacenews.com/bolden-details-trip-china-during-marshall-visit/>

Tasoff, Harrison. "Kilopower Project: NASA Pushes Nuclear Power for Deep-Space Missions," *Space.com*, January 22, 2018, available at <https://www.scientificamerican.com/article/nasa-pushes-for-nuclear-powered-space-missions/>

The Government of the Grand Duchy of Luxemburg. "Resources in Space," Space Resources.lu, available at <http://www.spaceresources.public.lu/en/about.html#>

The State Council Information Office of the People's Republic of China. "China's Space Activities in 2016," December 27, 2017, available at <http://english.scio.gov.cn/2017-01/10/content_40535777.htm>

The State Council of the People's Republic of China. "White Paper on China's Space Activities in 2016," December 28, 2016, available at <http://english.gov.cn/archive/white_paper/2016/12/28/content_281475527159496.htm>

The United States Congress, Office of Technology Assessment. *Ballistic Missile Defense Technologies* (Washington, DC: U.S. Government Printing Office, September 1985), available at <https://www.princeton.edu/~ota/disk2/1985/8504/850408.PDF>

The United States Department of Air Force. "America's Air Force Vision 2020," 2000, available at <http://webapp1.dlib.indiana.edu/virtual_disk_library/index.cgi/4240529/FID3869/pdfdocs/2020/afvision.pdf>

The United States Department of Defense. "Excerpts of Classified Nuclear Posture Review," *Nuclear Posture Review Report,* December 31, 2001, available at <https://fas.org/wp-content/uploads/media/Excerpts-of-Classified-Nuclear-Posture-Review.pdf>.

The White House. "National Space Policy of the United States of America," June 28, 2010, available at <https://www.nasa.gov/sites/default/files/national_space_policy_6-28-10.pdf>

The White House. "President Donald J. Trump Is Unveiling an America First National Space Strategy," March 23, 2018, available at <http://www.whitehouse.gov/briefings-

statements/president-donald-j-trump-unveiling-america-first-national-space-strategy/>

"Trump Budget Cuts U.S. Cash for International Space Station," *BBC*, February 12, 2018, available at <http://www.bbc.com/news/world-us-canada-43038329>

United Nations Committee on the Peaceful Uses of Outer Space. "Status of International Agreements relating to activities in outer space as at January 1, 2014," March 20, 2014, available at <http://www.unoosa.org/pdf/limited/c2/AC105_C2_2014_CRP07E.pdf>

United Nations General Assembly. "Preventing Outer Space Arms Race Would Avert Grave Danger; Possible New Verifiable Bilateral Multilateral Agreements Needed, Says Draft Text in First Committee," October 20, 2008, available at <https://www.un.org/press/en/2008/gadis3371.doc.htm>

United Nations Office for Disarmament Affairs. "Nuclear Weapons," available at <https://www.un.org/disarmament/wmd/nuclear/>

United Nations Office for Disarmament Affairs (UNODA). "Outer Space," available at <https://www.un.org/disarmament/topics/outerspace/>

United Nations Office for Outer Space Affairs, Inter-Agency Space Debris Coordination Committee. "IACD Space Guidelines," September 2007, available at <http://www.unoosa.org/documents/pdf/spacelaw/sd/IADC-2002-01-IADC-Space_Debris-Guidelines-Revision1.pdf>

United Nations Office for Outer Space Affairs. "United Nations Treaties and Principles on Outer Space, Related

General Assembly Resolutions and Other Documents," available at <http://www.unoosa.org/pdf/publications/ST_SPACE_061Rev01E.pdf>

Vedda, James. "Orbital Debris Remediation Through International Engagement," *Center for Space Policy and Strategy*, March 2017, available at <http://www.aerospace.org/wp-content/uploads/2017/09/DebrisRemediation.pdf>

Wall, Mike. "Asteroid Mining May Be a Reality by 2025," *Space.com*, August 11, 2015, accessible at <https://www.space.com/30213-asteroid-mining-planetary-resources-2025.html>

Weeden, Brian. "Space Weaponization: Aye or Nay?" *Arms Control Today*, November 4, 2008, available at <https://www.armscontrol.org/act/2008_11/Book_review>

Zonghuai, Qiao. "An Effective Way to Prevent an Arms Race in Outer Space the Early Negotiation and Conclusion of an International Legal Instrument," speech presented at the China/UN Disarmament Conference, April 3, 2002, available at <http://www3.fmprc.gov.cn/eng/29794.html>

About the Author

Ilayda is a curious and creative aspiring leader whose goal is to take and create opportunities that promote intelligent and sustainable solutions to business and policy challenges for a better future for all. She is a graduate of The Mahindra United World College of India ('14), and Colorado College ('18); a political science professional with a focus on international relations, an aerospace technologies and outer space policy enthusiast, and an avid traveler.

56684147R00047

Made in the USA
Middletown, DE
23 July 2019